3236

Music Minus One Clarinet

Piano Quintet in Eb Major, K.452

Wolfgang Amadeus Mozart - Quintet for Piano, Oboe, Clarinet, Horn and Bassoon in E-flat major, K. 452

Ludwig Van Beethoven - Quintet for Piano, Oboe, Clarinet, Horn and Bassoon in E-flat major, Op. 16

Mozart and Beethoven's Quintets for Piano and Winds can be grouped together as the only significant pieces of the Classical era that involve this particular instrumentation. Both quintets are popular and widely played staples of the repertoire. Given the rarity of this timbre, it is a novelty that the two most prominent figures of late eighteenth-century music decided to write these works. Exploring the similarities and differences between them enhances ones perspective on each.

Mozart completed his K. 452 just the day before its scheduled premiere at the National Court Theatre on April 1, 1784. Its success was immediate and, most importantly, Mozart himself was delighted with the sound of the work. His enthusiasm was overflowing in a letter to his father. "I consider it to be the best thing I have ever written". Interestingly enough, his next piece, the Piano Concerto in G Major, K. 453, involved extensive writing for the wind section.

Like Mozart's Quintet, the Opus 16 by Beethoven also received its premiere before a court, thirteen years later in 1797. Both composers played the piano parts at these first performances. Mozart was twenty-seven when he completed his Quintet, and Beethoven was twenty-six when he finished his. While Mozart had written 38 of his 41 symphonies, operatic works and more than half of his piano concerto at that age, Beethoven was just beginning to develop as a composer and his output contained only a handful of works. In fact, Beethoven did not arrive in Vienna from Bonn to make a name for himself as a composer until 1792, the year after Mozart's death. Two years before the premiere of Opus 16, Beethoven had just made his first public appearance in Vienna with the First and Second Piano Concerto.

Mozart's musical presence was still felt strongly in Vienna in 1792, and the young Beethoven must have experienced his remaining aura. It is possible that Beethoven chose to write a quintet with this particular instrumentation as homage to the great master. On the other hand, he may have been trying to distinguish himself to Mozart's admirers. Beethoven's decision to score the work in E-flat, the same key as Mozart's K. 452, further implies an awareness of the existing piece. Key relations between Mozart and Beethoven's work are prominent in several other instances. Mozart only wrote two piano concertos in minor keys: the D minor, K. 466 and the C minor, K. 491. Both works contain an intense drama and wide range of emotions. Beethoven went on to score the slow movement of his Opus 10 #3 Piano Sonata, and first movement of the Opus 31 #2 Piano Sonata in D minor with great affect in both. It is undeniable that C Minor later became an extremely powerful key to Beethoven. Both the Opus 13 and Opus 111 Piano Sonatas have first movements in this key.

Formally, both works fall comfortably into a standard, three-movement mold. The first movement of both pieces begins with a slow introduction before the faster tempo indication. In the slow movement of Mozart's Quintet, he writes in a very traditional ABA form. The middle movement of Opus 16 is in a ABACA rondo form. Each time the theme reappears, Beethoven makes it more ornate and complex. Incidentally, he chooses the same key for this movement as Mozart did - B-flat major. Both works contain a spirited Rondo as the final movement. A charming anecdote exists about Beethoven's premiere of his Rondo movement, in which he began to improvise during the fermata. He continued to do so with such fervor and excitement that the wind players grew restless with anticipation for their entrance. As they continued to raise their instruments up and down, their frustration worsened and the audience became increasingly delighted with the entire scene.

The difference in the two composers writing for the piano is substantial, foreboding the tremendous effect that Beethoven would eventually have on this instrument. Mozart writes more lyrically and he integrates the piano part with the wind parts more carefully, creating an equally balanced ensemble. Beethoven, on the other hand, treats the piano more as a soloist, exploiting the pianist's virtuosity. The rigorous passagework in the piano part is clearly a driving factor in shaping the piece.

The elegance, refinement and maturity of K.452 place it among any of Mozart's truly great chamber music pieces. The *Larghetto* movement in particular illustrates the exquisite nature of Mozart's melodic lines and harmonies. Beethoven's Opus 16, on the other hand, is most gratifying for its display of the composer's forward-thinking mind and innovative techniques. The use of abrupt dynamic swells and shifts as well as the intensity of the stormy writing allow us to hear a master in his early stages, developing a style which would define musical trends in the next century.

Liner notes by Jerry Wong

Printed in Canada

Mozart
Piano Quintet in Eb Major, K.452

Clarinet

LARGHETTO

RONDO
ALLEGRETTO

3236

Music Minus One

3236

Mozart
Piano Quintet in Eb major, K.452
- Clarinet -

Complete Version	Background Tracks	Movement Titles	Page No.
1	6	Largo	3
2	7	Allegro moderato	3
3	8	Larghetto...	4
4	9	Rondo - Allegretto	5
5		Tuning Notes - A440	

Music Minus One • 50 Executive Boulevard • Elmsford, New York 10523-1325
Website: www.musicminusone.com   Phone: 914-592-1188 • Fax: 914-592-3575

Music Minus One Clarinet

3236

Piano Quintet in Eb Major, K.452

Music Minus One • 50 Executive Boulevard • Elmsford, New York 10523-1325
Website: www.musicminusone.com   Phone: 914-592-1188 • Fax: 914-592-3575